Workbook

World Link
Developing English Fluency

Intro

HEINLE
CENGAGE Learning™

Australia • Brazil • Japan • Korea • Mexico • Singapore • Spain • United Kingdom • United States

World Link Intro Workbook
2nd Edition

Publisher: Sherrise Roehr

Senior Development Editor:
   Jennifer Meldrum

Senior Development Editor:
   Katherine Carroll

Director of Global Marketing:
   Ian Martin

Senior Product Marketing Manager:
   Katie Kelley

Assistant Marketing Manager:
   Anders Bylund

Content Project Manager:
   John Sarantakis

Senior Print Buyer:
   Mary Beth Hennebury

Composition: Pre-Press PMG

Cover/Text Design: Page2 LLC

Cover Image: iStockphoto

ISBN-13: 978-1-4240-6575-2
ISBN-10: 1-4240-6575-5

Heinle
20 Channel Center Street
Boston, MA 02210
USA

Cengage Learning is a leading provider of customized learning solutions with office locations around the globe, including Singapore, the United Kingdom, Australia, Mexico, Brazil, and Japan. Locate our local office at:
international.cengage.com/region

Cengage Learning products are represented in Canada by Nelson Education, Ltd.

Visit Heinle online at **elt.heinle.com**
Visit our corporate website at **cengage.com**

Printed in the United States of America
2 3 4 5 6 7 8 9 10 - 14 13 12 11

Photo Credits

Scope & Sequence

1 Greetings and Intros
Lesson A Getting to know you

1 Vocabulary Workout

A Complete the sentences. Use the words in the box.

Mr.	Smith	teacher	David

1. He is a _____.
2. His first name is _____.
3. His last name is _____.
4. In class, we call him _____ Smith.

B Match the words and numbers. Write the letter of the answer on the line.

1. seven _____	a. 2
2. four _____	b. 7
3. zero _____	c. 8
4. eight _____	d. 0
5. two _____	e. 4

C Complete the ID card. Use the words in the box.

Female	Last name	First name	Student	E-mail address

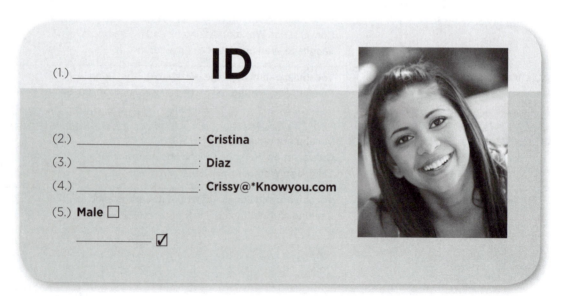

(1.) _____ **ID**

(2.) _____ : **Cristina**

(3.) _____ : **Diaz**

(4.) _____ : **Crissy@*Knowyou.com**

(5.) **Male** ☐

_____ ☑

2 Conversation Workout

A Number the sentences in order to make conversations.

1. _____ It's nice to meet you, Kenjiro.

   _____ Hi. What's your name?

   _____ Please call me Kenji. It's my nickname.

   _____ I'm Kenjiro.

2. _____ Hi. I'm Ming. Is Carlos your last name?

   _____ How do you spell Diaz?

   _____ Hello. I'm Carlos.

   _____ No, it's my first name. My last name is Diaz.

   _____ D-I-A-Z.

3. _____ Hmmm. You're not on my class roster.

   _____ Hi. My name is Yukiko.

   _____ Nice to meet you, Yukiko. My name is Mrs. Lane.

   _____ I'm a student in your class.

B Now write two more conversations.

1.

you: _____

your classmate: _____

you: _____

your classmate: _____

_____

2.

you: _____

your classmate: _____

you: _____

your classmate: _____

_____

3 Language Workout

A Complete the sentences. Use the words in the box.

am	is	are

1. It _____ my book.

2. She _____ the teacher.

3. I _____ Tina.

4. He _____ a soccer player.

5. You _____ a student.

B Rewrite the underlined sentences correctly.

1. She is a teacher. <u>My name is Mrs. Lee.</u>

   _____

2. You are my classmate. <u>Her first name is Linda.</u>

   _____

3. Carlos is a student. <u>Its last name is Diaz.</u>

   _____

4. I am a soccer player. <u>His name is John.</u>

   _____

5. Please call me Tino. <u>It's his nickname.</u>

   _____

C Rewrite the sentences. Use contractions.

1. She is my classmate.

   _____

2. It is an ID card.

   _____

3. I am your teacher.

   _____

4. He is a student.

   _____

5. You are in my class.

   _____

1 Vocabulary and Language Workout

A Match the questions and answers. Write the letter of the answer on the line.

1. Are you a teacher? _____	a. Yes, you are.
2. Is Rihanna a soccer player? _____	b. No, he isn't. He's from Cuba.
3. Is your phone number 555-4738? _____	c. Yes, it is.
4. Is your nickname Bill? _____	d. No, it isn't. It's Billy.
5. Is Carlos from Mexico? _____	e. No, she isn't. She's a singer.
6. Am I in your class? _____	f. No, it isn't. It's my name tag.
7. Is this your ID card? _____	g. No, I'm not. I'm a student.

B Complete the chart with your information. Then answer the questions.

Full name	Francis (Frank) Hong	Susan (Sue) Parker	Raquel (Rocky) Sanchez	You
Phone number	(513) 555-0318	(267) 555-1334	(987) 555-1758	
E-mail address	FHong@*gotnet.com	SSP@*boing.com	RSan@*comm.com	
Favorite actor	Bruce Lee	Penelope Cruz	Leonardo DiCaprio	

Example: Is Susan's phone number (267) 555-1758? *No, it isn't. It's (267) 555-1334.*

1. Is Susan's nickname Sue? _____

2. Is Raquel's e-mail address RSan@*boing.com? _____

3. Is Frank's favorite actor Penelope Cruz? _____

4. Is Francis's nickname Frankie? _____

5. Is Rocky's phone number (987) 555-1758 _____

6. Is your favorite actor Leonardo DiCaprio? _____

7. Is your nickname Buddy? _____

2 Reading and Writing

A Read the article.

English nicknames

His real name is William Arthur Philip Louis of Wales, but his family calls him Wills.

His real name is Henry Charles Albert David of Wales, but everyone calls him Prince Harry.

Nicknames are very popular in English!

Some nicknames are female. Cathy is a nickname for Catherine. Sue is a nickname for Susan. Liz, Lizzie, Beth, Bess, and Betty are all nicknames for Elizabeth.

Men also have nicknames. Bob and Rob are nicknames for Robert, and Mike is a nickname for Michael.

Some nicknames are male and female. Chris is a nickname for Christine. It's also a nickname for Christopher.

What's your nickname?

B Write short answers.

1. Is Michael a nickname? _____

2. Are Liz and Cathy female nicknames? _____

3. Is Beth a female name? _____

4. Is Sue a nickname for Elizabeth? _____

5. Are nicknames popular in your country? _____

C Write the nicknames next to the names.

Male names	Nickname	Female names	Nickname
1. Robert	_____	**4.** Susan	_____
2. Michael	_____	**5.** Elizabeth	_____
3. Christopher	_____	**6.** Catherine	_____

D Circle the correct answer.

His name (1.) (am / **is** / are) Yoshihiko Sato. Everyone (2.) (**calls** / what's / meets) him Yoshi.

(3.) (**He's** / His / Him) a student. (4.) (He's / **His** / Him) phone numbers is (631) 555-8763. His e-mail

(5.) (name / number / **address**) is sato85@*nihon.net. His favorite (6.) (**sports player** / show / book)

is Lionel Messi.

E Draw a picture of your friend. Then write about him or her.

2 Countries and Nationalities

Lesson A Countries of the world

1 Vocabulary Workout

A Circle the correct answer.

1. Yusuf is from Ankara, (Turkish / Turkey).

2. Luis is from (Brazil / Brazilian).

3. Mei Li is (China / Chinese).

4. The capital of (Japanese / Japan) is Tokyo.

5. Hyun Ji is from Seoul. She is (Korea / Korean).

6. Ryan is from Canberra. He's (Australian / Australia).

B Complete the sentences with the correct language.

1. John is from London.
   He speaks _____.

2. I am Japanese.
   I speak _____.

3. Monica is from Mexico City.
   She speaks _____.

4. Maria is Brazilian.
   She speaks _____.

5. Ali is from Turkey.
   He speaks _____.

6. In Korea, people speak _____.

C Match the words that go together. Write the letter of the answer on the line.

1. Beijing _____	a. capital
2. Mandarin _____	b. country
3. Australian _____	c. language
4. Mexico _____	d. nationality

2 Conversation Workout

A   Complete the conversations.

1. **China / Shanghai**

   A: Where are you _____?

   B: I'm Chinese. _____ from Shanghai.

   A: Is that the capital of _____?

   B: No, it _____. Beijing is the capital.

2. **Colombia / Bogota**

   A: Where _____ _____ _____?

   B: I'm Colombian. I'm from Bogota.

   A: _____ _____ _____ capital _____ _____?

   B: Yes, _____ _____

3. **Germany / Munich**

   A: _____

   B: _____

   A: _____

   B: _____

B   Match the words that go together. Write the letter of the answer on the line.

1. Where are _____	a. China?
2. Which _____	b. exactly?
3. Are you _____	c. you from?
4. Whereabouts in _____	d. from China?
5. Where _____	e. city?

3 Language Workout

A Choose the correct word or contraction to complete each sentence. Write the letter of the answer on the line.

1. Hello? Hello? _____ is this?

    a. Who's

    b. Where

    c. Who

2. _____ are you?

    a. Who's

    b. Where

    c. Where's

3. You're in France? _____ in France?

    a. Where

    b. Where's

    c. Who's

4. _____ with you?

    a. Where

    b. Who

    c. Who's

B Complete the conversation. Use *in*, *at*, and *from*.

A: Oh, Maria! Hello. Where are you?

B: I'm (1.) _____ Mexico. Lisa is with me.

A: Who's Lisa? Where is she (2.) _____?

B: She's my Australian friend. She's (3.) _____ Sydney. We're (4.) _____ the beach today.

A: And where is this beach?

B: It's (5.) _____ Cancun. It's really beautiful!

C Complete the sentences. Use the words in the box.

Who	Who's	Where's	in	at

1. _____ is this?

2. _____ your school?

3. Are you _____ home now?

4. _____ with you?

5. Is Alan _____ New York?

Lesson B What is your city like?

1 Vocabulary and Language Workout

A Write the adjectives for cities in the chart. Use your opinions.

beautiful	old	ugly	expensive	boring	safe
quiet	big	interesting	noisy	modern	crowded
fun	small	inexpensive	deserted	dangerous	

It's good. ☺	It's OK. 😐	It's bad. ☹

B What's it like? Write sentences. Give your own ideas for the last two.

Example: New York City ___*New York City is crowded and expensive.*___

1. Mexico City _____

2. Tokyo _____

3. Paris _____

4. Los Angeles _____

5. _____ _____

6. _____ _____

C Write sentences. Use *is*, *isn't*, *are*, and *aren't* with an adjective in the box.

old	beautiful	noisy	~~boring~~	safe	deserted

Example: My town isn't interesting. ___*It's boring*___

1. The streets aren't crowded. _____

2. My town isn't modern. _____

3. The streets are quiet. _____

4. It is dangerous. _____

5. The town isn't ugly. _____

2 Reading and Writing

A Read the article. Match these cities with the descriptions in the article: Brasilia, Rome, Oxford, New York.

park

museum

building

Name the City

1. _____
This is a very big city! It's in North America. There are many museums and art galleries. It's expensive but it's interesting.

2. _____
It's a new capital. It's in South America. The buildings are big and modern. There are many parks.

3. _____
This is a small, quiet English city. There's a very old university and 16,000 students from many countries live here.

4. _____
This city is very old. It's crowded and noisy, but the buildings are very beautiful. There are lots of interesting neighborhoods.

B Answer the questions. Use your own opinions.

1. Which city is good for a vacation? _____

2. Why? _____

3. Which city is bad for a vacation? _____

4. Why? _____

C Read this travel ad. Cross out the seven spelling mistakes. Write the correct spelling above them. The first one is done for you.

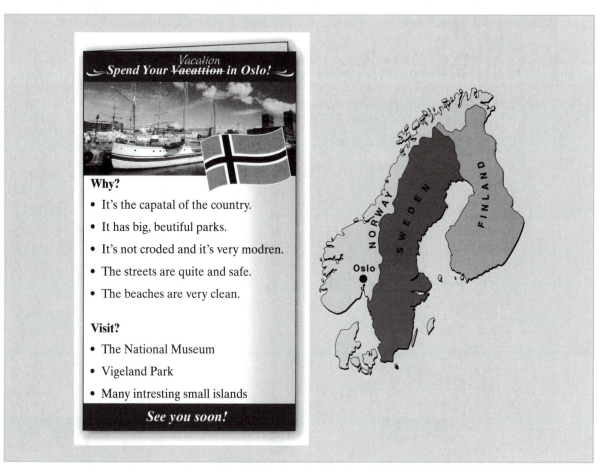

Vacation
Spend Your ~~Vacattion~~ in Oslo!

Why?

- It's the capatal of the country.
- It has big, beutiful parks.
- It's not croded and it's very modren.
- The streets are quite and safe.
- The beaches are very clean.

Visit?

- The National Museum
- Vigeland Park
- Many intresting small islands

See you soon!

D Now write a travel ad for your favorite city.

1 Vocabulary Workout

A Match the sentence halves. Write the letter of the answer on the line.

1. I can't find my digital _____.
2. This is Alice's photo _____.
3. That's a pretty pair of _____.
4. I have an MP3 player with _____.
5. This is Bill's graduation _____.
6. That is a beautiful cell _____.
7. We have two gift _____.
8. That is an expensive DVD _____.

a. headphones
b. earrings
c. player
d. camera
e. cards
f. album
g. gift
h. phone

B Look at the photos. Unscramble the words.

h r b i d y a t   n g r d a u t a i o   d w i d n g e

_____   _____   _____

C Answer these questions.

1. What is your favorite personal item?   _____

2. Is it expensive or inexpensive?   _____

3. Is it a gift from a friend?   _____

2 Conversation Workout

A Circle the correct phrase to complete each conversation.

1. **A:** Thanks so much!

   B: Excuse me. / No problem. / No, it isn't.

2. **A:** Who is it? / Is this your dictionary? / What's your name?

   B: Yes, it is. Thanks!

3. **A:** Is that your laptop? / Thanks for the gift. / What's this?

   B: You're welcome.

4. **A:** Thank you. / Excuse me. / Are these your earrings?

   B: No, they aren't.

5. **A:** Thanks so much. / Excuse me. / It's an MP3 player.

   B: My pleasure.

6. **A:** Sure, no problem. / Wow! What's this? / Is this your cell phone?

   B: No, it isn't.

B Write your own conversations.

1. **A:** _____

   B: _____

   A: My pleasure.

2. **A:** _____

   B: _____

3. **A:** Excuse me. _____

   B: _____

   A: _____

4. **A:** Is this your _____ ?

   B: _____

5. **A:** _____

   B: No problem.

3 Language Workout

A Write the plurals.

1. MP3 player _____

2. country _____

3. camera _____

4. cell phone _____

5. dish _____

6. dictionary _____

7. TV _____

8. watch _____

9. key _____

10. capital _____

B Write each word in the correct box.

MP3 player	sunglasses	dictionary	pictures
city	author	actor	e-mail address
watches	teacher	headphones	ID card
exercise	friends	music	TV

a	an	—
city	exercise	sunglasses

C Write questions and answers.

Example: sunglasses   _What are these?_   _They're sunglasses._

1. a birthday gift   _____   _____

2. earrings   _____   _____

3. a watch   _____   _____

4. an ID card   _____   _____

5. headphones   _____   _____

Lesson B Keepsakes

1 Vocabulary and Language Workout

A Write the opposite of each word.

1. important_____
2. common_____
3. uncool_____
4. unusual_____
5. expensive_____
6. popular_____
7. bad_____
8. first_____

B Unscramble the sentences.

1. gift / it / an / is / expensive

_____

2. digital / album / photo / is / that / a

_____

3. unusual / these / earrings / are

_____

4. camera / gift / nice / a / is / a

_____

5. common / a / Smith / name / is / last

_____

6. music / cool / is / that

_____

C Look around the room. Write sentences using the words in Exercise A.

Example: *Those are unusual shoes.*

1. _____
2. _____
3. _____
4. _____
5. _____
6. _____

2 Reading and Writing

A Read this catalog page and fill in the products. The first one is done for you.

New Products from Sunny Electronics!

Example: _TV_____

The BG-124. Get a very big picture at a very small price.

1. _____
The MUS-65—Enjoy cool headphones with this popular new way to play music.

2. _____
The beautiful new LC-009. Have fun with games and the Internet and e-mail your friends. $5,000.

3. _____
Talk to your friends. Take pictures. Send text messages.
The CL-260. Everyone has one. Only $90.

4. _____
The DC-1000. Use it for birthdays, graduations, and weddings.
Take beautiful pictures. Only $250.

B Circle _T_ for _true_ and _F_ for _false_. Rewrite the false sentences to make them true.

1. The BG-124 is small.   T   F

_____

2. The MUS-65 is uncool.   T   F

_____

3. The LC-009 is expensive.   T   F

_____

4. The CL-260 is uncommon.   T   F

_____

5. DC-1000 pictures are terrible.   T   F

_____

C Read this e-mail. Some words are scrambled. Unscramble them.

Date: 10/2   Subject: Cameras for you   From: spacey@*flash.net   To: ben@*lsp.com

Hi Ben!

My new (1.) reamac _____ is great! It's a brand-new (2.) crudtop _____ from Sunny. It's called the CD260. It's (3.) sunulua _____ (none of my friends have it) and a little (4.) nepsiveex _____ (about $500) but the pictures are so beautiful. I think it's an (5.) entlexlec _____ camera.

See you!
Chris

D Write an e-mail to your friend about your favorite electronic product.

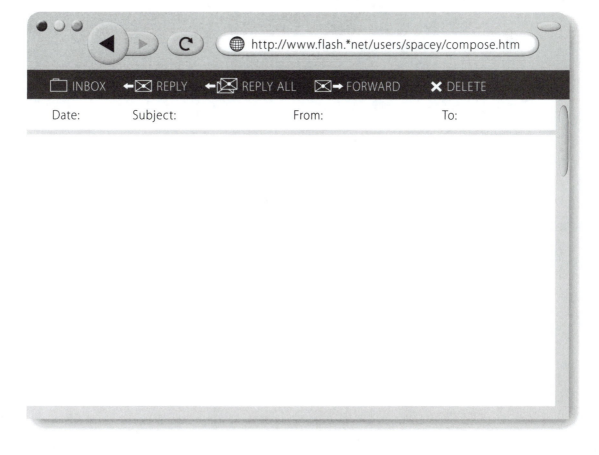

Date: Subject: From: To:

4 Activities and Interests

Lesson A Everyday activities

1 Vocabulary Workout

A Unscramble the words.

1. c h a t w __ __ __ __ __ ing
2. n i s t l e __ __ __ __ __ __ ing
3. k a l t __ __ __ __ ing
4. t t x e __ __ __ __ ing
5. s c e r e i x __ __ __ __ __ __ __ __ ing
6. k i n r d __ __ __ __ __ ing
7. t i w a __ __ __ __ ing
8. d y s u t __ __ __ __ __ ing

B Complete each sentence with the correct preposition. Use *to, for,* or *on.* Write Ø if no preposition is needed.

Example: She is eating ___Ø___ breakfast now.

1. They are studying _____ a test.
2. He is eating _____ a hamburger.
3. She is waiting _____ a bus.
4. Tina is texting _____ her sister.
5. Uncle Marco is talking _____ the phone.
6. He is talking _____ his son.
7. Ming is listening _____ music.
8. We are studying _____ math.

C Complete the sentences with the correct form of one of the verbs in the box.

wait	listen	eat	drink	talk	watch

1. Ali is _____ to her friends.
2. They are _____ lunch in a restaurant.
3. She is _____ a movie.
4. Pedro is _____ to his MP3.
5. Dad is _____ coffee.
6. Linda is _____ for her sister.

2 Conversation Workout

A Number the sentences in order to make a conversation.

_____ Sorry to hear that.

_____ Hi, Hiro. How're you doing?

_____ So-so.

____1____ Hello?

_____ Hey, Tina. It's Hiro.

_____ Fine. How about you?

_____ Yeah? What's wrong?

_____ I'm studying for a test and don't understand the chapter.

B Write a conversation like the one in activity A. Use your own ideas.

A: _____

B: _____

A: _____

B: _____

A: _____

B: _____

A: _____

B: _____

3 Language Workout

A Write sentences. Use the present continuous.

Example: Elena / play the guitar _____*Elena is playing the guitar.*_____

1. Carlos / write e-mail _____

2. They / listen to music _____

3. Susan / talk on her cell phone _____

4. We / eat pizza _____

5. Min-chul / watch TV _____

B Make the sentences negative.

Example: She's reading.   _She is not reading._

1. He is sleeping.   _____

2. You are studying hard.   _____

3. Sally is talking to her partner.   _____

4. We are watching TV.   _____

5. I am texting my brother.   _____

C Write questions.

Example: you / cook dinner   _Are you cooking dinner?_

1. John / play tennis   _____

2. she / listen to music   _____

3. Mr. and Mrs. Sosa / exercise   _____

4. you / watch a movie   _____

5. we / learn English   _____

D Look at the company schedule and answer the questions.

Mega Corporation Today, Monday June 4

Daily Schedule

Staff	Task
Frank	Answer letters
Linda & Claudia	Meet with Mr. Pak
Joe	Read e-mail messages
Rosa	Talk to new customers
David	Write reports
Ahmed	Answer phones
Olivia	Work at the computer

1. What's Frank doing today?   _____

2. Is Joe reading e-mail messages?   _____

3. What's Rosa doing today?   _____

4. What are Linda and Claudia doing?   _____

5. Is David writing letters today?   _____

6. Who is answering the phones?   _____

7. Is Olivia meeting with Mr. Pak?   _____

8. What is Olivia doing today?   _____

Lesson B At school

1 Vocabulary and Language Workout

A Unscramble the names of these school subjects. One letter is already in each word.

1. gnitwir	w __ __ __ __ __ __		6. sniglEh	__ __ g __ __ __ __
2. hamt	__ __ __ h		7. rat	__ __ t
3. ccsniee	__ c __ __ __ __ __		8. snubsies	__ u __ __ __ __ __ __
4. roysthi	__ __ __ __ __ __ y		9. gnieegnreni	__ __ __ __ __ __ __ __ __ __ g
5. realittrue	l __ __ __ __ __ __ __ __ __		10. scumi	m __ __ __ __

B Write the subjects for each kind of school. Use words from Activity A, as well as your own ideas. You can use some words more than once.

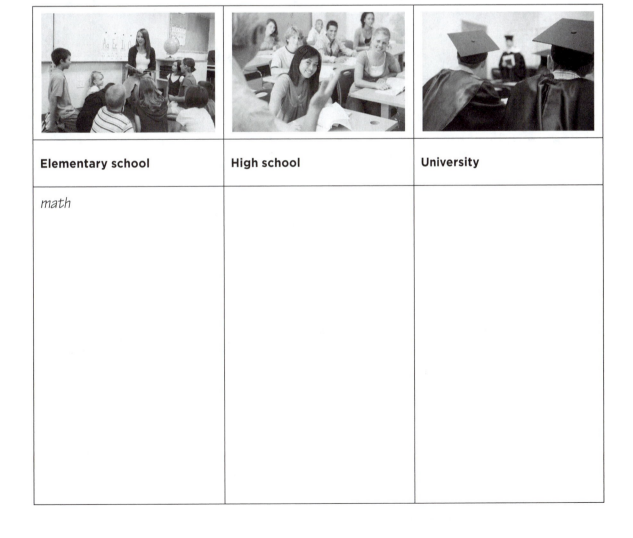

Elementary school	High school	University
math		

2 Reading and Writing

A Read this article from a university newspaper.

Student Life

International Students Enjoy Summer

Hiroko

"I'm from Osaka, Japan. I'm majoring in computer science, but this summer I'm just studying English—six hours a day! Also, I joined the tennis club, and I'm playing tennis every day. It's great. I'm meeting lots of Americans."

Felix

"I'm from Berlin, the capital of Germany. My major is North American Studies. This summer, I'm taking three classes at the university—U.S. history, American literature, and English. I'm really busy! After class, I like listening to music."

Gisele

"I'm from Sao Paulo, Brazil, and I'm an art major. I'm taking two art classes in summer school. There is a lot of homework. I'm working very hard this summer! To relax, I'm taking a yoga class."

B Complete the chart with information from the article.

Name	Nationality	Major	Subjects	Free Time
	Japanese			
		North American Studies		
				yoga

C Read this vacation postcard. Fill in the verbs in the correct form.

Dear Lisa,

Hello from Rome. I'm here with Elena. Right now, we're _____ in a great little cafe near the Colosseum. We're _____ coffee and _____ ice cream. This summer, we're _____ around Europe. We're _____ lots of interesting cities like Paris and Berlin. And, of course, we're _____ for clothes. We're not _____ very much. What about you? Are you _____ hard?

See you!

Cathy

PLACE STAMP HERE

D Now imagine your vacation. Draw a picture and write a postcard to your friend.

PLACE STAMP HERE

1 Vocabulary Workout

A Complete the sentences. Use the words in the box.

dinner	breakfast	salad	spaghetti	eat	drink	lunch	milk	dessert

1. I have _____ at 6:00 in the morning.
2. I _____ toast and I _____ coffee.
3. I eat _____ at school at 12:00.
4. I have soup and a _____, and I drink _____ with it.
5. I eat _____ at home at 7:00 in the evening.
6. My favorite meal is _____ with tomato sauce.
7. For _____, I like cake and ice cream.

B Write sentences about what you eat and drink.

Example: *I have lunch at work. I eat fish and soup.* _____

1. _____
2. _____
3. _____
4. _____
5. _____

C Write your favorite foods in the chart below.

breakfast	
lunch	
dinner	
dessert	
drinks	

2 Conversation Workout

A Put the sentences in the correct order to make conversations.

1. Are you hungry? / Let's go to China Garden. They have great food. / Yes, I love it. / Yes, I am. Do you like Chinese food? / OK, let's go there.

   Sue: _____

   Alex: _____

   Sue: _____

   Alex: _____

   Sue: _____

2. That's OK. They have chicken and pasta, too. / Sounds good! / Well, I don't really like pizza. / Let's go to Pizza Paradise for dinner.

   Anna: _____

   Pilar: _____

   Anna: _____

   Pilar: _____

3. Then let's go to Tito's Mexican Restaurant. / I'm hungry, too. Let's have dinner. / Do you like tacos? / I'm hungry! / Yes, I like them a lot.

   Hiroshi: _____

   Ken: _____

   Hiroshi: _____

   Ken: _____

   Hiroshi: _____

B Now write your own conversation.

   A: _____

   B: _____

   A: _____

   B: _____

   A: _____

3 Language Workout

A Choose the correct verb for each sentence. Make sure you use the correct form. Pay attention to spelling.

drink	speak	do	have	study	go

1. We _____ toast and coffee for breakfast.
2. Laura _____ three languages: English, French, and Spanish.
3. I _____ my homework every day.
4. The students _____ to the library.
5. Nami _____ five cups of tea every day.
6. Man-Ho _____ math and computer science.

B Make the sentences negative.

1. I eat breakfast every day.   _____
2. Carmen speaks Japanese.   _____
3. We like tests.   _____
4. Young-Mi drinks coffee.   _____
5. My friends study a lot.   _____
6. I sleep in class.   _____

C Write true sentences with these verbs.

Example: play   *I play the guitar.* _____

About you:

1. like   _____
2. eat   _____
3. speak   _____

About your friend: (Name: _____)

4. have   _____
5. go   _____
6. study   _____

Lesson B Food and health

1 Vocabulary and Language Workout

A Choose the correct word for each sentence.

diet	energy	lose	spicy	junk	salty	sweet

1. A diet helps you _____ weight.
2. Ice cream tastes _____.
3. French fries are usually _____.
4. The food you eat gives you _____.
5. Another word for "hot" is "_____".
6. If you eat very little, you are on a _____.
7. Food that is not healthy is _____ food.

B Write questions and short answers. Use the words in parentheses.

Example: (you / like / spicy food)   *Do you like spicy food?* _____

　　　　　　(yes)   *Yes, I do.* _____

1. (your mother / cook / every day)   _____

　　(no)   _____

2. (your friends / take / vitamins)   _____

　　(yes)   _____

3. (French fries / taste / good)   _____

　　(yes)   _____

4. (I / eat / junk food)   _____

　　(no)   _____

5. (fruit / taste / salty)   _____

　　(no)   _____

C Write questions and answers about people you know. Use *like* and different foods.

Example: (_Marta_)   **Q:** *Does Marta like pizza?* _____

　　　　　　　　　　　A: *Yes, she does* _____

1. (_____)   **Q:** _____

　　　　　　　　A: _____

2. (_____)   **Q:** _____

　　　　　　　　A: _____

3. (_____)   **Q:** _____

　　　　　　　　A: _____

2 Reading and Writing

A Read the article. Write the correct number for each picture.

What's your diet like?

1. I live in Istanbul, Turkey. My favorite food is ice cream. I also like cookies and cake. I eat too much junk food, but it's so delicious! I also like some healthy foods, especially yogurt and beans. I eat any food that tastes good to me.

—Ali Aslan

2. I eat only healthy foods like vegetable soup and rice dishes. I also eat a lot of chicken. In Japan, it's easy to find foods like these. I don't drink fruit juice or soda—just bottled water. Do I like eating this way? No, I don't. But I need to lose weight. I'm on a diet.

—Kenji Ono

3. I take a lot of vitamins. I want to be healthy so I also watch what I eat. Mostly I have salads—fruit salad, vegetable salad, chicken salad—any salad is fine with me. I live in Mexico, but I never eat tacos. And I never eat junk food. Sometimes I have smoothies. They're sweet and delicious. They're also good for me.

—Marta Diaz

B Complete the chart.

Name	Country	Foods	Why?
			They're delicious. They taste good.
Kenji Ono			
		salads smoothies	

C Put the verbs in the correct form.

My health habits are good. I (1. eat)_____ breakfast
everyday. I (2. not, smoke)_____, and I (3. not,
drink)_____ beer. I (4. exercise)_____ a lot,
and I (5. play)_____ tennis. I (6. not, eat)_____
a lot of junk food, but I (7. love)_____ ice cream. I
(8. sleep)_____ eight hours every night.   I (9. take)
_____ care of my health.
Toshi (10. be)_____ my best friend. He's very
different from me. Toshi (11. not, take)_____ care of
his health. He (12. smoke) _____ a lot, and he (13. not,
exercise) _____. He (14. not, eat) _____
breakfast. He (15. eat)_____ junk food all day. He
(16. study)_____ very hard, and he (17. sleep)
_____ four hours every night. I'm worried about Toshi!

D Write sentences about your health habits. Are they good ☺, OK ☺, or not so good ☹?

6 My Family

Lesson A This is my family!

1 Vocabulary Workout

A Write each word in the correct box.

father   wife   sister   parent   son

mom   brother   grandfather   grandmother   dad

grandparent   mother   husband   daughter

Male	Female	Male or Female

B Match the sentence parts. Write the letter of the answer on the line.

1. Your mother's father is your _____.	a. mother
2. Your sister's mother is your _____.	b. parents
3. Your son's sister is your _____.	c. son
4. Your father's mother is your _____.	d. grandfather
5. Your mother and father are your _____.	e. mom
6. Another word for mother is _____.	f. twins
7. Your husband's son is your _____.	g. daughter
8. Two children born together are _____.	h. grandmother

C Your turn! Describe your family.

Example: *I have two brothers. Nino is 16 years old. Alex is 10 years old.*

_____

_____

_____

_____

2 Conversation Workout

A A reporter is looking at a picture and talking
with Lori Smith about her family. Put the words in order.

1. (this / person / who / is)

   _____?

2. (my / sister / that's / father's)

   _____.

3. (brothers' / what / names / are / your)

   _____?

4. (Jason / their / names / Matt / and / are)

   _____.

5. (names / parents' / are / your / what)

   _____?

6. (Sally / my / mother's / Paul / name / and / is / name / is / father's / my)

   _____

   _____.

7. (sister's / name / what's / your)

   _____?

8. (Lisa / name / is / her)

   _____.

B Your turn. Write an interview about your family.

Reporter: _____

_____

You: _____

_____

Reporter: _____

_____

You: _____

_____

Reporter: _____

_____

You: _____

_____

3 Language Workout

A Read the chart and complete the sentences with the owners' names.

Do you have a / an . . . ?	Charles	Shelly	The Parks
MP3 player	no	yes	no
computer	yes (this year!)	no	yes (six years old)
car	no	yes (Ford)	yes (Toyota)
cell phone	yes	no	no
guitar	no	yes	no
dog	yes (name; Rex)	no	yes (name: Blackie)

1. Blackie is _____ dog.

2. _____ computer is new.

3. _____ car is Japanese.

4. _____ MP3 player is nice.

5. Where is _____ cell phone?

6. I like _____ guitar.

B Complete the sentences. Use the names in the picture.

1. Sarah is _____ wife.

   She is _____ grandmother.

2. Annie is _____ sister.

   She is _____ daughter.

3. Kayla is _____ daughter.

   She is _____ granddaughter.

   She is also _____ granddaughter.

4. Jeff is _____ husband.

   He is _____ brother.

   He is also _____ father.

C Change the sentences. Use *his, her,* or *their.*

Example: Pablo is Marina's brother.   *Pablo is her brother.*

1. My grandfather's house is small.   _____

2. My sister's name is Akiko.   _____

3. John's parents are divorced.   _____

4. My daughters' names are Cathy and Wendy.   _____

5. I'm Ali's cousin.   _____

6. This is my brother's car.   _____

Lesson B Family relationships

1 Vocabulary and Language Workout

A   Unscramble these words.

1. emridra   _____

2. ginsel   _____

3. edricovd   _____

4. denchril   _____

5. derynifob   _____

6. geenis monoese   _____

7. rengridfli   _____

B   Write the conversation. Unscramble the sentences.

1. (born / you / were / where)

   A: _____?

2. (born / in / was / Colombia / I)

   B: _____.

3. (old / you / are / how)

   A: _____?

4. (years / I / am / old / 23)

   B: _____.

5. (you / single / are)

   A: _____?

6. (children / no / married / am / and / have / I / I / two)

   B: _____.

C   Write the numbers in words.

Example: 153   _one hundred fifty-three_ _____

1. 77   _____

2. 380   _____

3. 46   _____

4. 525   _____

5. 3,200   _____

6. 604   _____

7. 9,030   _____

8. 5,280   _____

2 Reading and Writing

A What's your opinion? Circle your answers.

1. Large families are happy families.	Yes	Maybe	No
2. Children need two parents.	Yes	Maybe	No
3. Twins are very lucky.	Yes	Maybe	No
4. I want a lot of children.	Yes	Maybe	No

Star Talk

This week in Star Talk...
Actress Liza Naylor talks about her four husbands!

"Yes, it's true… I married my first husband in 1979 in London. I was too young. Nigel and I have two sons. Now Ian and Derek live in England."

"I married Raymond in Los Angeles in 1987. He's an actor—a bad actor! But we have a beautiful daughter. Her name is Lily. She lives with her father and her stepmother."

"In 1996, I married James in Sydney. We have two children. Jason and Jenny are twins. James is a good man, but he's the wrong husband for me. His new wife is a famous scientist."

"I'm so happy now! I have a wonderful life with my husband, Pierre. I married Pierre in 2003. This is true love! We have a new baby. His name is Luc. I live in a big house in Switzerland with Pierre, my baby, the twins, and Pierre's three daughters. Their names are Zelda, Zenia, and Zora. I love big families!"

B Read the article about Liza Naylor. Then complete the sentences with words from the box. There are two extra words.

mother	father	sister	son	grandmother	daughter	brother

1. Zora is Zelda's _____.

2. Liza is Lily's _____.

3. Ian is Liza's _____.

4. Pierre is Zora's _____.

5. Derek is Ian's _____.

C Write the year in words.

Example: 1993   *nineteen ninety-three*

1. 2002   _____

2. 1979   _____

3. 2025   _____

4. 1987   _____

5. this year   _____

D Read and complete the paragraph. Use possessive nouns.

The Douglas Family

(Grandparents)	**Kirk**	**Diana** (first wife)
		Anne (current wife)
(Parents)	**Michael**	**Diandra** (first wife)
		Catherine (current wife)
(Grandchild)	**Cameron**	

Michael Douglas is an American actor. His movie *It Runs in the Family* is very interesting. It's about a family with many problems—and the actors are (1.) _____ real family. Kirk Douglas, (2.) _____ real father, plays Michael's father and (3.) _____ grandfather in the movie. (4.) _____ first wife, Diana, plays his wife in the movie, too. Michael plays (5.) _____ father in the movie, and Cameron plays (6.) _____ son, and (7.) _____ and Diana's grandson. Some Douglas family actors weren't in the movie. (8.) _____ current wife, Catherine, wasn't in it because of her new baby. The Douglas family wants to make more movies together.

E Write about a family in a movie or TV show. Who are the actors? What are the characters like?

_____
_____
_____
_____
_____
_____
_____
_____
_____
_____
_____
_____

7 Time

Lesson A Time and schedules

1 Vocabulary Workout

A Write these times in numbers.

1. a quarter to seven _____	5. two thirty _____
2. one thirty _____	6. a quarter to four _____
3. midnight _____	7. five o'clock _____
4. a quarter after ten _____	8. nine oh five _____

B Match the times (1–8) with the clocks (a–h).

1. six thirty

2. a quarter to seven

3. three ten

4. noon

5. a quarter after eleven

6. seven thirty

7. four oh eight

8. one forty-five

a   b   c   d

e   f   g   h

C Put these times in order from earliest to latest.

midnight	evening	noon	night	afternoon	morning

→ _____ → _____ → _____

→ _____ → _____ → ___*midnight*___

D What time do you . . . ? Write the times in numbers and words. Follow the example.

Example: eat dinner   _7:30   seven thirty_____

1. get up   _____

2. eat breakfast   _____

3. start English class   _____

4. finish English class   _____

5. watch your favorite TV show _____

2 Conversation Workout

A Make suggestions. Follow the example.

Example: the Pizza Palace   _Let's have dinner at the Pizza Palace._

1. the new Disney movie   _____

2. swimming   _____

3. Cafe Colombia   _____

4. the Metro Shopping Center   _____

5. *The Evening News* at 7:00   _____

B Answer with *I don't really ... .* Follow the example.

Example: Let's listen to some piano music.

I don't really like piano music.   OR   _I don't really want to listen to music._

1. Let's watch a basketball game on TV.

_____

2. Let's play tennis.

_____

3. Let's see the new Liza Naylor movie.

_____

4. Let's eat at Joe's Restaurant.

_____

5. Let's go shopping.

_____

C Complete the conversations.

1. **Julia:** _____ go to the new Chinese restaurant.

   Janice: _____ . I don't _____ .

   Julia: _____ Japanese food.

   Janice: _____ sounds _____ !

2. **Ken:** _____ play _____ .

   Chris: Hmmmm . . . _____ .

   Ken: Then _____ .

   Chris: OK, _____ !

D Write your own conversation.

A: _____

B: _____

A: _____

B: _____

3 Language Workout

A Write *in, on,* or *at.*

1. Marco has English class _____ Thursday _____ 8:00 _____ the morning.
2. I work in a department store every day _____ the afternoon.
3. I always watch the news on TV _____ 7:00 _____ the evening.
4. _____ Saturday, I always get up _____ 10:00.
5. Hassan visits his grandparents _____ Friday evenings.
6. Our math exam is _____ 4:30 _____ Tuesday.

B This is a work schedule at a store. Write sentences about these people. Follow the example.

	Monday	Tuesday	Wednesday	Thursday	Friday	Saturday
morning	Mimi	Jack	Jack	Jack	Jack	Jane
afternoon	David	Ann	Mimi	Fred	David	Jane
evening	Sam	x	Sam	x	Sam	Sam

Example: Jack _____ *He works in the morning.* _____

1. Mimi _____
2. Ann _____
3. Jane _____
4. Sam _____
5. Fred _____
6. David _____

C Write *on, in, at, from,* or *to.*

1. My English class is _____ 9:00 _____ 10:00 on Tuesday and Thursday.
2. I usually study _____ the afternoon.
3. I go home _____ 4:00.
4. I watch TV _____ 5:00 _____ 6:00.
5. I don't study at all _____ Saturday.

D Read the answers. Then write *when* questions. Follow the example.

Example: Q: *When is your favorite show on TV?*   **A:** My favorite show is on TV at 6:00 tonight.

1. **Q:** _____   **A:** My piano lesson is at 3:00 on Tuesday.
2. **Q:** _____   **A:** The test is at 2:00 on Friday.
3. **Q:** _____   **A:** The party is on Saturday night.
4. **Q:** _____   **A:** Jim's dance class is at noon tomorrow.

1 Vocabulary and Language Workout

A Write the weekend activities with words from the box.

in	shopping	family	a day off	with friends	the movies

1. go _____
2. go to _____
3. go out _____
4. sleep _____
5. spend time with your _____
6. take _____

B Write lists of weekend activities. Use phrases from **A** as well as your own ideas.

I love to... 😊	It's OK to... 😐	I don't like to... 😞

C Write the questions. Use *what* or *where*.

1. **Q:** _____   **A:** On weekends, I study and see my friends.
2. **Q:** _____   **A:** I live on Lake Street.
3. **Q:** _____   **A:** I go to the library after class.
4. **Q:** _____   **A:** I have a sandwich and coffee for lunch.
5. **Q:** _____   **A:** I go to Baxter School.
6. **Q:** _____   **A:** I study history.

2 Reading and Writing

A Read the interview and write the questions from the box in the correct spaces.

The Life of Wade Evans

> Who do you live with?
>
> When do you relax?
>
> What do you do in your free time?
>
> Where do you live?
>
> What do you do on Saturday?
>
> What do you do in the evening?

Wade Evans is an international tennis star. Our reporter talks to Wade about his life.

Reporter: _____?

Evans: I have a big house in California. The weather is very good for tennis.

Reporter: _____?

Evans: I live with my dog. His name is Racket.

Reporter: _____?

Evans: Free time? What's that? I work out at the gym in the morning for two hours. Then I play tennis for four hours.

Reporter: _____?

Evans: I watch sports on TV, and I answer my e-mail. People ask me a lot of questions about tennis.

Reporter: _____?

Evans: I work hard on Saturday. I play tennis for six hours and then I watch tennis videos.

Reporter: _____?

Evans: I relax on Sunday. I have lunch with my parents and see my girlfriend.

B Write *T* for *true* or *F* for *false*. Rewrite the false sentences to make them true.

1. Wade relaxes every day.   T   F

   _____

2. He plays tennis on Sunday.   T   F

   _____

3. He has a computer.   T   F

   _____

4. He spends time with his parents on Saturday.   T   F

   _____

5. He answers questions about tennis.   T   F

   _____

6. He lives with his parents.   T   F

   _____

C Read this interview. Fill in the spaces with *in*, *on*, or *at*.

Student Weekly: INTERVIEWS

Our reporter is talking to famous singer Dottie LaVelle.

Reporter: What do you do to relax?
Dottie: Well, (1.) _____ the evening, I play with my children. I'm a single parent. My daughter is six, and my son is three. They go to bed (2.) _____ 8:00. Then I read or watch movies. (3.) _____ Mondays and Wednesdays (4.) _____ 7:00, I take an art class. Really! I'm learning how to draw.

Reporter: What about weekends?
Dottie: I usually work (5.) _____ Friday and Saturday nights. I have a concert or a live TV show. (6.) _____ the afternoon, I practice singing. (7.) _____ the morning, I sleep very late. My children stay with their grandmother (8.) _____ the weekends.

D Imagine you are a famous person. Answer the reporter's questions.

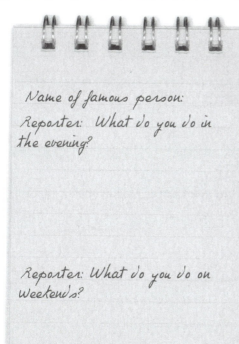

Name of famous person:
Reporter: What do you do in the evening?

Reporter: What do you do on weekends?

8 Special Occasions

Lesson A Holidays and celebrations

1 Vocabulary Workout

A Complete the names of the months.

1. __ a __	7. F __ __ __ u __ __ __
2. __ __ __ __ h	8. A __ __ __ l
3. __ __ __ e	9. S __ __ __ __ __ __ __ r
4. __ __ __ y	10. __ __ __ u __ __ __
5. A __ __ __ __ __	11. O __ __ __ __ __ r
6. __ __ v __ __ __ e __	12. D __ __ __ __ __ __ __

B Write the ordinal numbers for the days of the months. Follow the example.

Example: 12/10 _December tenth_

1. 2/16 _____

2. 8/23 _____

3. 11/9 _____

4. 10/1 _____

5. 4/5 _____

6. 7/4 _____

7. 6/27 _____

8. 3/10 _____

C Write down five important holidays. Use numbers and then words. Follow the example.

Example: _New Year's Day_ _1/1_ _January first_

Important Holidays:

1. _____ _____ _____

2. _____ _____ _____

3. _____ _____ _____

4. _____ _____ _____

5. _____ _____ _____

2 Conversation Workout

A Number the sentences in order to make a conversation.

_____ It's a holiday in the United States.

_____ Sounds interesting. Do people do anything special?

_____ Really? When is it?

_____ Do you have plans for Memorial Day?

_____ Yes. They usually have barbecues.

_____ Memorial Day?

_____ It's the last Monday in May.

B Put the words in order to make statements and questions.

1. (have / we / day / the / off)

   _____

2. (last / in / Friday / the / June / it's)

   _____

3. (do /on / do / people / what / day / this)

   _____

4. (weekend / a / long / it's)

   _____

5. (a / U.S. / here / it's / the / holiday / in)

   _____

C Match the expressions with the percentages.

1. I don't really know. _____	a. 100% sure
2. It's on May 20th. _____	b. 50 % sure
3. It could be. _____	c. 0% sure

D Write a conversation about a holiday.

A: _____

B: _____

A: _____

B: _____

A: _____

B: _____

3 Language Workout

A Complete the paragraph with *in* or *on*.

Five people in my family have birthdays (1.) _____ the spring. Two birthdays are (2.) _____ April. My birthday is (3.) _____ April 16th and my mother's birthday is (4.) _____ April 20th. There are three birthdays (5.) _____ May.

My father's birthday is (6.) _____ May 1st, my grandfather's birthday is (7.) _____ May 3rd, and my sister's birthday is on May 11th. We have one big birthday party for all the birthdays (8.) _____ the spring. My brother is different. His birthday is (9.) _____ the fall, (10.) _____ October 12th. He's lucky. We have a party just for him!

B Write sentences. Follow the example.

Example: my birthday / July 10   *My birthday is on July tenth.* _____

1. our vacation / summer   _____

2. our party / New Year's Day   _____

3. Labor Day / September   _____

4. Valentine's Day / winter   _____

5. Christmas / December 25   _____

C Write *C* if the sentence is *correct*. Write *I* if it is *incorrect*. Cross out the mistakes and correct them.

1. _____ On Saturday, I work in the morning.

2. _____ My English class is in Wednesday at 8:00 in the evening.

3. _____ In the summer, I go swimming, and on the winter, I go skiing.

4. _____ In Japan, classes start in April.

5. _____ My grandmother's birthday is on July 12th. She was born on 1927.

6. _____ The class party is at 2:00 in the afternoon on Friday.

1 Vocabulary and Language Workout

A Complete the paragraph. Use the words in the box.

attend	event	take	traditional	place	annual	miss

Thousands of people (1.) _____ the Sundance Film festival every year. It takes

(2.) _____ in Park City, Utah. This (3.) _____ festival happens

every January and it's the biggest (4.) _____ of the year in Park City. People

(5.) _____ photos of their favorite actors and actresses. Big, expensive parties

are a (6.) _____ part of the festival. No moviemaker or actor wants to

(7.) _____ Sundance.

B Match the things that go together.

It's a ...

1. They go to the Olympics. _____   a. film festival
2. They show movies. _____   b. food festival
3. They listen to singers. _____   c. sports festival
4. They make unusual meals. _____   d. music festival

C Complete the sentences with *in, on, at, from, to, until,* or *for.*

1. They play soccer _____ two hours every day.

2. The movie starts _____ 8:00.

3. The party is _____ 9:00 _____ 12:00.

4. I don't have classes _____ Sunday.

5. School closes _____ the summer.

6. The winter holiday lasts _____ ten days.

7. The festival runs _____ Monday _____ Friday.

8. I stay with my grandparents _____ two weeks every summer.

2 Reading and Writing

A Read the website and write the correct letter for each picture.

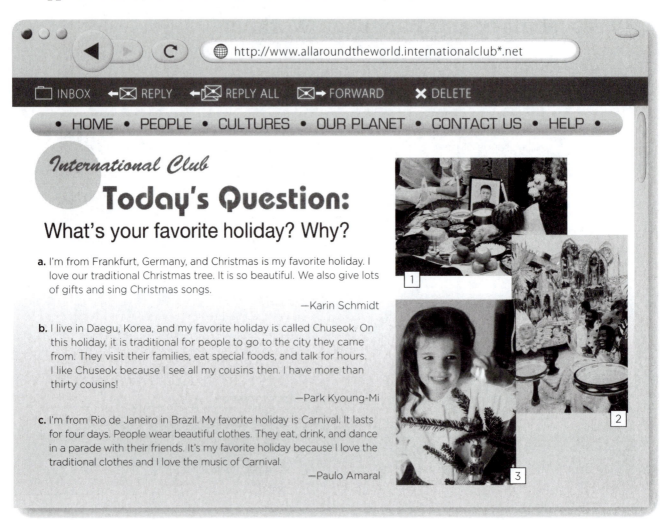

http://www.allaroundtheworld.internationalclub*.net

☐ INBOX   ←✉ REPLY   ←✉ REPLY ALL   ✉→ FORWARD   ✖ DELETE

• HOME • PEOPLE • CULTURES • OUR PLANET • CONTACT US • HELP •

International Club

Today's Question:
What's your favorite holiday? Why?

a. I'm from Frankfurt, Germany, and Christmas is my favorite holiday. I love our traditional Christmas tree. It is so beautiful. We also give lots of gifts and sing Christmas songs.

—Karin Schmidt

b. I live in Daegu, Korea, and my favorite holiday is called Chuseok. On this holiday, it is traditional for people to go to the city they came from. They visit their families, eat special foods, and talk for hours. I like Chuseok because I see all my cousins then. I have more than thirty cousins!

—Park Kyoung-Mi

c. I'm from Rio de Janeiro in Brazil. My favorite holiday is Carnival. It lasts for four days. People wear beautiful clothes. They eat, drink, and dance in a parade with their friends. It's my favorite holiday because I love the traditional clothes and I love the music of Carnival.

—Paulo Amaral

B Fill in the chart.

Name	Country	Favorite Holiday	Why?
1.			He sees all of his cousins.
2.			
3.			

C Read about a favorite holiday. Cross out the eight spelling mistakes. Rewrite the misspelled words correctly on the lines below.

I'm from Oslo, Norway. My favorite ~~holliday~~ takes palce anualy on May 17th. That's our National Day here in Norway. We sing special songs for this day. All the cities have big parades. The school children preform songs and their parents watch. The children also go to the houses of old people and sing for them. The largest parade is in Oslo. About a hundred thousand people atend this parade. The people waer traditionel clothes. For me, it's the most interesting evint of the year.

1. _holiday_   3. _____   5. _____   7. _____

2. _____   4. _____   6. _____   8. _____

D What's your favorite holiday? Why? What special activities do you do on that day?

My favorite holiday is . . . _____

_____

_____

_____

_____

_____

_____

_____

9 Person to Person

Lesson A Living with others

1 Vocabulary Workout

A Complete each sentence with the correct form of the verb *do* or *make*.

1. When we need food, I _____ the grocery shopping with my mother.

2. Every morning I _____ my bed.

3. My mother _____ the most money.

4. I usually _____ a snack for myself after school.

5. Sometimes my sister _____ an appointment to talk to her teacher.

6. I usually _____ the dishes after dinner.

7. I have a part-time job so I can _____ money for clothes.

8. My father usually _____ some chores on Saturday morning.

B Read and complete the paragraph. Use the present tense or present continuous form of *make* or *do*.

My mother has a job so my brother and I help her at home. We (1.) _____ a lot of chores every day. First, I (2.) _____ the beds. Then I (3.) _____ the breakfast dishes. My brother takes out the garbage. Right now I (4.) _____ the laundry. I (5.) _____ my homework at the same time. My brother is talking on his cell phone. He (6.) _____ plans to see his girlfriend.

C Who does each job in your house? Write the person's name after the job. You can write more than one name after a job.

does the dishes _____

makes breakfast _____

takes out the garbage _____

does the laundry _____

cleans the bathroom _____

2 Conversation Workout

A Unscramble the sentences.

1. sorry / about / I'm / that _____

2. worry / it / don't / about _____

3. I'm / sorry / really _____

4. OK / that's _____

5. all right / that's _____

B Write each sentence from **A** in the correct row.

Apologizing	_____ _____ _____
Responding to an apology	_____ _____ _____

C Your turn. Write a conversation in which someone apologizes. You can use the conversation on **student book** page 92 as a model.

Martin: _____

Gail: _____

Martin: _____

Gail: _____

Martin: _____

Gail: _____

Martin: _____

Gail: _____

3 Language Workout

A Look at the survey and write sentences. Follow the example.

	Max	Jane	Toshi	Anna
Do you get up early?	sometimes	always	often	never
Do you eat breakfast?	always	never	always	usually
Are you late for class?	sometimes	hardly ever	never	sometimes
Do you drink coffee?	often	sometimes	never	never
Are you a good student?	sometimes	sometimes	usually	usually

Example: Anna / get up early   _Anna never gets up early._

1. Max / drink coffee   _____

2. Max and Toshi / eat breakfast   _____

3. Anna / good student   _____

4. Toshi and Anna / drink coffee   _____

5. Anna and Max / late for class   _____

6. Jane / eat breakfast   _____

7. Jane / late for class   _____

8. Toshi / get up early   _____

B What about you? Answer with a frequency adverb.

1. Do you get up early?   _____

2. Do you eat junk food?   _____

3. Are you usually late for class?   _____

4. Do you drink tea?   _____

5. Do you go to bed late?   _____

6. Do you eat breakfast at home?   _____

C Write sentences. Follow the example.

Example: usually   _We usually have a test on Friday._

1. always   _____

2. hardly ever   _____

3. sometimes   _____

4. often   _____

5. never   _____

6. usually   _____

Lesson B Modern dating

1 Vocabulary and Language Workout

A Match each sentence starter with the correct ending. Write the letter of the answer on the line.

1. If you never met the person before, _____	a. it is a perfect date.
2. If each person pays half, _____	b. is *guy.*
3. If you are having a wonderful time, _____	c. you split the bill.
4. If you are with the same person for six months, _____	d. you ask them out.
5. Another word for *man* _____	e. you are a couple.
6. If you ask someone to go on a date, _____	f. it is a first date.
7. If you go out with a person for the first time, _____	g. it is a blind date.
8. If you pay for two dinners, _____	h. you pick up the check.

B Complete the questions with *who, where,* or *what.*

1. A: _____ is that?   B: That's my friend, Ina.

2. A: _____ is the movie?   B: It's at the Rialto.

3. A: _____ are those boys?   B: They're my brothers.

4. A: _____ is in the bag?   B: My books.

5. A: _____ is Luis?   B: He's at work right now.

6. A: _____ do you go on dates?   B: We usually go to a dance club.

7. A: _____ pays for the dates?   B: We usually split the bill.

8. A: _____ do you go on a first date?   B: We usually go to a coffee shop.

C Unscramble the words to make questions. Then write true answers.

1. you / where / do / go / class / after _____

_____

2. eat / lunch / what / do / you / for _____

_____

3. who / well / speaks / very / English _____

_____

4. you / where / to / do / school / go _____

_____

5. do / what / you / on / Sunday / do _____

_____

2 Reading and Writing

A Read this web page.

> http://worldlinkkeypals*.net
>
> 📁 INBOX   ←✉ REPLY   ←✉ REPLY ALL   ✉→ FORWARD   ✖ DELETE
>
> **Key-pals are e-mail friends. They write e-mails and send photos. Do you want a key-pal? Complete this form. Then check your e-mail every day!**
>
> | | |
> |---|---|
> | **Name:** | Catherine Leclaire **Age:** 19 |
> | **E-mail:** | calec@*wow.net |
> | **Hometown:** | Montreal, Canada |
> | **Hobbies:** | I like movies, music, and reading books from many countries. |
> | **Daily life:** | I'm a university student. I'm studying history. On weekends, I work in a restaurant. It's fun! |
>
> | | |
> |---|---|
> | **Name:** | Ayako Yamamoto **Age:** I'm 13. |
> | **E-mail:** | ayachan@*sugoi.com |
> | **Hometown:** | I live in Sapporo, Japan. |
> | **Hobbies:** | My hobbies are music, cartoons, and shopping. |
> | **Daily life:** | I go to school from 8:00 to 4:00. Then I go shopping and watch TV. I sometimes study in the evening — sometimes! |
>
> | | |
> |---|---|
> | **Name:** | Becky Travis **Age:** 17 |
> | **E-mail:** | becky@*floridatel.com |
> | **Hometown:** | My hometown is Miami, Florida, in the USA. |
> | **Hobbies:** | I love tennis, volleyball, and soccer. |
> | **Daily life:** | I'm a student at Miami High School, I play on my school volleyball team in winter, and I play on the soccer team in summer. |
>
> | | |
> |---|---|
> | **Name:** | Eliana Santos **Age:** 20 |
> | **E-mail:** | e_santos@*sol.net |
> | **Hometown:** | I'm from Sao Paulo, Brazil. |
> | **Hobbies:** | Swimming, reading, music, watching movies |
> | **Daily life:** | I work in an office from Monday to Friday. On weekends, I usually take a trip somewhere. |

B Now answer these questions about the web page.

1. Who lives in Brazil? _____

2. What is Catherine's job? _____

3. Where does Becky live? _____

4. Who works in an office? _____

5. What are Ayako's hobbies? _____

6. Who likes sports? _____

7. Who is a good match for Catherine? _____

   Why? _____

C Write the information in the box in the correct place.

Seoul, Korea	music	basketball
Monday to Friday: study at Central University	Min Song-Gyu	drawing
Saturday and Sunday: work in a dance club	songgyu@*han.com	20

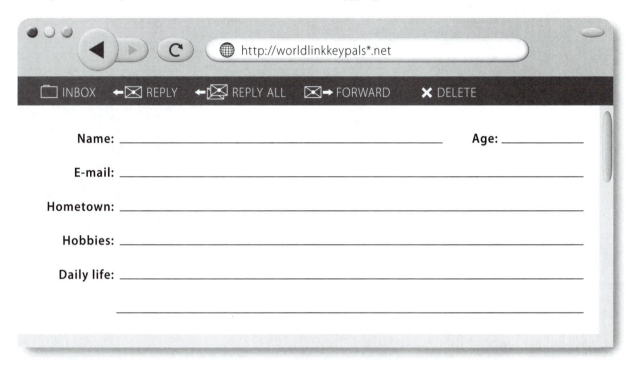

D Now write your information on the key-pal form.

10 Home Sweet Home

Lesson A Housing

1 Vocabulary Workout

A Match the room with the description. Write the letter of the answer on the line.

1. elevator _____
2. balcony _____
3. kitchen _____
4. garage _____
5. bathroom _____
6. bedroom _____
7. living room _____
8. yard _____

a. You wash dishes there.
b. You wash your hair there.
c. You put a sofa there.
d. It goes up and down.
e. You sleep there.
f. It is an outdoor area behind a house.
g. It is a part of the house, but outdoors.
h. You keep your car there.

B Complete the sentences. Use the words in the box.

air conditioner	closet	table	window	refrigerator	washing machine

1. Please put the clean clothes in the bedroom _____.
2. Put your dirty clothes in the _____.
3. I'm too warm. Please turn on the _____.
4. I don't like the noise in the street. Please close the _____.
5. Please put the plates and cups on the _____.
6. Please put the milk in the _____.

C What items are in these rooms in your house? Make a list.

1. Living room: _____

   _____

2. Kitchen: _____

   _____

3. Bedroom: _____

   _____

2 Conversation Workout

A Complete the conversation.

Max: Hi, Tranh.

Tranh: Hi, Max. _____ in.

Max: Thanks. So, this is your new place. _____ nice apartment!

Tranh: Yeah, and _____ $600 a month.

Max: _____? 600? That's cheap.

Tranh: Yeah, and there's free Internet.

Max: _____.

Tranh: It's true. _____ great apartment. _____ just one problem.

Max: What's that?

Tranh: _____ air-conditioning.

B Now write conversations about these pictures. Use your own ideas.

You: Hi, _____.

Your friend: Hi, _____. Come in.

You: Thanks. So, _____ your new _____.

Your friend: Yeah, and it's only _____.

You: No way. _____? That's _____.

Your friend: Yeah, and there's _____.

You: For real?

Your friend: It's true. It's a great _____. _____ just one problem.

You: What's that?

Your friend: There's no _____.

You: Hi, _____.

Your friend: Hi, _____. Come in.

You: _____. So, this is your new _____.

Your friend: Yeah, and it's only _____.

You: You're joking. _____? That's _____.

Your friend: Yeah, and there's _____.

You: For real?

Your friend: It's true. It's a great _____. There's just one _____.

You: What's that?

Your friend: There's no _____.

3 Language Workout

A Write questions and answers about Yasuo's living room. Follow the example.

Example: _Is there_ _____ a sofa in the living room? _Yes, there is._ _____

1. _____ a TV? _____
2. _____ windows? _____
3. _____ a table? _____
4. _____ a computer? _____
5. _____ chairs? _____
6. _____ a rug? _____

B Write sentences about your bedroom. Follow the example.

Example: _There is a bed._ _____

1. _____ 4. _____
2. _____ 5. _____
3. _____ 6. _____

C Make questions and write answers that are true for you. Follow the example.

Example: _How many rooms are there in your apartment?_ _____

There are four. _____

1. people / your family _____

_____

2. pages / this book _____

_____

3. students / your class _____

_____

4. windows / your bedroom _____

_____

5. units / this book _____

_____

Lesson B Decorate a room

1 Vocabulary and Language Workout

A Circle the correct word in each sentence.

Example: Look at those ((white) / blue) clouds.

1. The leaves of plants are usually (pink / green).

2. The sky is (brown / blue).

3. Linda's eyes are (brown / yellow).

4. My grandfather's hair is (dark blue / dark gray).

5. When you mix red and white, you get (purple / pink).

6. A person's eyes are never (orange / brown).

7. When you mix black and white, you get (green / gray).

8. In the fall, the leaves on the trees turn (blue / orange).

9. Dogs never have (light pink / dark brown) hair.

10. The morning sunlight looks (black / yellow).

B Rewrite the underlined sentences correctly. Use *very, too,* or *really.* If the sentence is correct, write C.

Example: I worked 10 hours today. I'm very tired to go out.

I'm too tired to go out.

1. Lisa is too nice. She always helps people.

   _____

2. Bob can't stop jumping around. He's very excited to sit down.

   _____

3. I can't eat anything. I'm really worried about the test.

   _____

4. Ali is very rich. His family has a lot of money.

   _____

5. The baby is too young. She's only ten days old.

   _____

6. Fatima is 70 years old. She's too old to ride a bicycle.

   _____

7. Elementary school students can't vote. They're very young.

   _____

8. I can't go to the party tonight. I'm really busy to go.

   _____

2 Reading and Writing

A Skim the article very quickly. Who writes about each of these colors?

1. yellow   _____

2. blue   _____

3. green   _____

B Read the newspaper column.

How the Color of our Walls Affects Us

Emily Lawson
Interior Decorator

Blue is one of my favorite colors. **It** can really change how a room feels. Light blue walls make people feel calm. However, dark blue has a very different effect. **It** often makes people feel sad and depressed. Most decorators love light blue, but **others** can't stand it.

Bruce Fieldson
Psychologist

I tell all my clients to avoid painting their rooms yellow. This color seems to stimulate the nervous system. Babies cry more in a yellow room, and people are more likely to lose their temper there than in blue or green rooms. Some scientists also think that it causes the eyes to get tired faster when reading.

Pamela Geer
Office Manager

I always paint the walls in the office where I work light green. It helps people feel relaxed and at ease. Researchers have also found that green helps people read better. If you put a transparent green paper over the page of a book, you will read faster. That's good in an office, too.

C Find the meaning for each pronoun.

1. The first word **it** in Emily Lawson's part means _____.

2. The second word **it** in Emily Lawson's part means _____.

3. The word **others** in Emily Lawson's part means other _____.

D Read the description of an apartment. Circle the names of rooms. Underline the names of colors.

I love my apartment. The living room is a big, square room. I painted it bright yellow. There is a dark blue sofa. Across from it are two big red chairs. There's a white plastic table between the sofa and the chairs.

The dining table is in the dining room. It is painted bright red. There is a dark green rug under the table.

My bedroom is very restful and relaxing. The walls are light blue. There are three windows on one wall so the room is always very bright.

The kitchen walls are white. The refrigerator and other appliances are white, too. There's a tiny microwave on the counter and a big table in the middle of the room. I always keep some bright yellow flowers on the table.

E Reread D. Then rewrite the description of the apartment. Make it a place you would like to live in. Change the rooms, furniture, and colors to ones you would like. Use your own ideas. You can add new items if you wish.

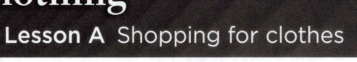

11 Clothing

Lesson A Shopping for clothes

1 Vocabulary Workout

A Use the letters to write the names of clothing.

1. h i t s r   _____
2. s e r s d   _____
3. o l l u p r e v _____

4. t a c k e j _____
5. t o a c   _____
6. f r c s a   _____

B Write the clothing words in the correct column in the chart.

| pants | scarf | shorts | boots | heels | sandals |
| gloves | jeans | hat | skirt | socks | sneakers |

For Your Head	For Your Feet	For Your Legs	For Your Hands

C Describe clothing that you own. Tell the color of each item.

Example: *I have brown boots.* _____

1. _____
2. _____
3. _____
4. _____
5. _____
6. _____

2 Conversation Workout

A Name one object and one item of clothing for each color. Follow the example.

Example: red: _tomatoes, my T-shirt_____

1. blue: _____
2. green: _____
3. white: _____
4. yellow: _____

B Ming and Lisa are shopping. Complete the conversations.

1. **Clerk:** _____ you?

    Ming: Oh, yeah, _____. I'm _____ for a gift for a friend.

    Clerk: Well, _____ these nice silk scarves. This one is from Italy.

    Ming: How much _____?

    Clerk: Fifty dollars.

    Ming: I'll think _____.

    Clerk: You can buy this red wool scarf for fifteen dollars.

    Ming: It's nice. I'll _____.

2. **Clerk:** May I _____?

    Lisa: Oh, yeah, _____. I'm _____ a gift for my brother.

    Clerk: Well, _____ these nice gloves. They're from France.

    Lisa: How much _____?

    Clerk: Forty dollars.

    Lisa: I'll think _____.

    Clerk: You can buy these wool socks for five dollars.

    Lisa: They're nice. _____.

C Write a conversation between yourself and a clerk in a clothing store.

Clerk: _____?

You: Oh, yeah, _____. _____.

Clerk: _____.

You: _____?

Clerk: _____.

You: _____.

Clerk: _____.

You: It's nice. _____.

3 Language Workout

A Use the words to make sentences.

Example: scarf / want / you / buy / do / this / to (question)
Do you want to buy this scarf?

1. has / T-shirt / he / new / a

_____

2. go / they / mall / the / want / to / to

_____

3. shoes / want / he / new / doesn't

_____

4. she / want / hat / for / pay / does / to / $20 / that (question)

_____

B Circle the correct word or words.

Example: I don't have boots. I (have / (have to)) buy some.

1. I don't (want / want to) go shopping today.
2. My sister (has / has to) three pairs of heels.
3. They (want / want to) some new clothes.
4. We (have / have to) a lot of clothing stores in our town.
5. Do you (want / want to) get new shoes?
6. Erica (doesn't want / doesn't want to) any new clothes.
7. You (don't have / don't have to) buy that belt.
8. The clerk (has / has to) work all day.
9. My mother (wants / wants to) a new coat.
10. Michael (doesn't want / doesn't want to) pay $15 for that hat.

C Complete the sentences. Use your own ideas.

1. I want _____.
2. I want to _____.
3. (My friend) _____ wants to _____.
4. (My friend) _____ wants _____.
5. I have _____.
6. I have to _____.
7. (My friend) _____ has to _____.
8. (My friend) _____ has _____.

1 Vocabulary and Language Workout

A Match the sentence halves. Write the letter of the answer on the line.

1. T-shirts usually _____

2. If you are warm, _____

3. After exercising, I always _____

4. A hat will _____

5. Before you buy that jacket, _____

6. These gloves are too small. They _____

7. If you are too cool, _____

8. Jackets always _____

a. put on a sweater.

b. take off your sweater.

c. have long sleeves.

d. protect your head from the sun.

e. try it on.

f. have short sleeves.

g. don't fit.

h. change clothes.

B Identify the underlined word. Write *C* for *count noun* and *N* for *noncount noun*.

_____ 1. I need to buy some new clothes.

_____ 2. Where did you buy those boots?

_____ 3. What is the price of that shirt?

_____ 4. That necklace is my favorite piece of jewelry.

_____ 5. Wearing new clothes is a lot of fun.

_____ 6. That skirt is really cool.

_____ 7. New clothing can be expensive.

_____ 8. Do you own a pair of sandals?

C Circle the correct answer.

Example: Did you study (a / an / —) history last night?

1. I like (a / an / —) clothing from Italy.

2. He is trying on (a / an / —) suit.

3. My mother lost (a / an / —) earring.

4. I spend (a / an / —) time at the mall every weekend.

5. I have to get (a / an / —) new hat.

6. Do you want (a / an / —) long-sleeve shirt?

2 Reading and Writing

A Match the people with their clothes.

What are you wearing at work today?

a. I'm wearing a white blouse, a white skirt, and white shoes. My hat is also white. My clothes are always very clean.

b. I'm wearing dark blue pants and a light blue shirt. I'm also wearing a big dark blue hat and black shoes.

c. I'm wearing green and yellow shorts and a green and yellow shirt. My sneakers are yellow, and my socks are green. Sometimes my clothes are dirty.

d. I'm wearing old jeans and an old red shirt. My hat is brown and very, very big.

e. Today I'm wearing a purple jacket, a pink blouse, and a blue skirt. I'm also wearing purple shoes, and my bag is pink. My clothes are always very beautiful.

1. A policeman _____

2. A model _____

3. A soccer player _____

4. A nurse _____

5. A cowboy _____

B Jinny Kim is talking about her favorite party clothes. Fill in the blanks with *a* or *an*. Write *X* in the blanks that don't need *a* or *an*.

I usually wear (1) _____ casual clothes to (2) _____ party. I wear (3) _____ t-shirt and (4) _____ jeans, or I sometimes wear (5) _____ skirt. And I love (6) _____ jewelry. I always wear (7) _____ earrings, (8) _____ necklace, and (9) _____ big rings.

C What are your favorite party clothes? Write your answers.

1 Vocabulary Workout

A Use the letters to write the names of jobs.

1. c r o d o t _____
2. r e w a l y _____
3. s u r n e _____
4. t r a w i e _____
5. m o g m e p r r r a _____
6. d s i n e g r e _____

B Complete the sentences. Use the words in the box.

receptionist	cashier	flight attendant	housewife	dentist
hairstylist	waitress	police officer	chef	tutor

1. A _____ helps keep people safe on the street.
2. A _____ is a doctor for your teeth.
3. A _____ can help you pass your exams.
4. A _____ sits near the front door of an office.
5. A _____ tries to make people look good.
6. A _____ takes your money in a store.
7. A _____ cooks food in a restaurant.
8. A _____ works in an airplane
9. A _____ works at home.
10. A _____ serves food in a restaurant.

C Write the names of friends and family members. Tell what job they do.

Name	Job
1. _____	_____
2. _____	_____
3. _____	_____
4. _____	_____
5. _____	_____

2 Conversation Workout

A Number the sentences to make a conversation.

_____ I'm a waitress at Jamie's.

_____ Hi, Jack. I'm Anna.

_____ Yeah, that's me. But I don't work in the library anymore.

___1___ Hi. Are you a friend of Linda's?

_____ Really? What do you do now?

_____ I like it a lot and the money's really good.

_____ Yeah, hi. My name is Jack.

_____ Anna ... I know you. You're Linda's friend, too, right? You work in the library.

_____ What's that like?

B *Today* magazine is interviewing people about their jobs. Complete the interview.

Reporter: _____?

Wendy: I'm Wendy Chang.

Reporter: Where _____?

Wendy: _____ Chang's Driving School.

Reporter: What _____?

Wendy: I'm a driving instructor. I teach people to drive.

Reporter: _____?

Wendy: Yes, I like my job a lot.

Reporter: _____ your students like?

Wendy: They're very friendly.

C Write another interview. The reporter is interviewing your friend.

Reporter: _____

Your friend: _____

Reporter: _____

Your friend: _____

Reporter: _____

Your friend: _____

Reporter: _____

Your friend: _____

Reporter: _____

Your friend: _____

3 Language Workout

A Rewrite the sentences as questions. Use the words *what* and *like*.

Example: Tell me about Alice.

What's she like?

1. I work in an animal hospital.

_____

2. You haven't met my brother yet.

_____

3. My art teacher is Mrs. Granger.

_____

4. I work six days a week.

_____

5. I've met a lot of new people this year.

_____

B Complete the conversations. Add a question with the word *like*.

Example: **A:** Chris has a job at the police department.

B: _What's that like?_

A: Well, sometimes the work is dangerous.

1. **A:** I almost never see my parents anymore.

B: _____

A: They're nice, but they don't understand me very well.

2. **A:** My boyfriend is from Mexico.

B: _____

A: He's very talkative.

3. **A:** My new doctor is only 22 years old.

B: _____

A: She's very intelligent.

4. **A:** I work at a candy factory.

B: _____

A: It's pretty boring most of the time.

Lesson B Getting a job

1 Vocabulary and Language Workout

A Match the sentence halves. Write the letter of the answer on the line.

1. One of a teacher's responsibilities _____
2. An engineering job _____
3. She doesn't get any pay because she _____
4. One of the requirements for the job _____
5. The new boss _____
6. A singer _____
7. Every student who finishes college _____
8. Every course you take _____

a. has a lot of experience.
b. is a college education.
c. must have musical skills.
d. gets a degree.
e. is to correct tests.
f. is a volunteer.
g. requires a background in math.
h. improves your skills.

B Can you do these things? Write *yes* or *no*. What about your friend?

	Speak German	Use a Computer	Paint	Play Basketball
You				
Your friend				

C Now write sentences with *can* or *can't*. Use the information from the chart above.

1. I _____ speak German.
2. _____
3. _____
4. _____

5. My friend _____ speak German.
6. _____
7. _____
8. _____

D Complete the conversation. Linda Starr is an actress. She wants a job in a new movie.

Mrs. Lee: So, Linda, _____ can you do? _____ _____ sing?

Linda: Yes, I _____ sing a _____ bit, but not very well.

Mrs. Lee: Hmmm. _____ _____ dance?

Linda: I _____ dance a _____ _____.

Mrs. Lee: Hmm. You _____ sing or dance very _____. _____ you cry?

Linda: Oh, yes! I _____ _____ very well.

Mrs. Lee: That's great! Our new movie is *Lost Love.* You can do the job!

2 Reading and Writing

A Marisol is writing to her new key-pal. Scan her message and circle the three questions.

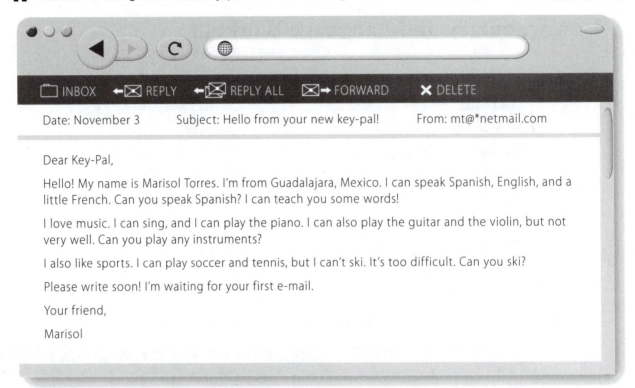

INBOX   REPLY   REPLY ALL   FORWARD   DELETE

Date: November 3   Subject: Hello from your new key-pal!   From: mt@*netmail.com

Dear Key-Pal,

Hello! My name is Marisol Torres. I'm from Guadalajara, Mexico. I can speak Spanish, English, and a little French. Can you speak Spanish? I can teach you some words!

I love music. I can sing, and I can play the piano. I can also play the guitar and the violin, but not very well. Can you play any instruments?

I also like sports. I can play soccer and tennis, but I can't ski. It's too difficult. Can you ski?

Please write soon! I'm waiting for your first e-mail.

Your friend,

Marisol

B What can Marisol do? Check (✓) the correct answers.

	yes	a little	no
1. sing			
2. speak French			
3. play tennis			
4. ski			
5. play the piano			
6. speak English			
7. play soccer			
8. play the violin			

C Read this e-mail and fill in the spaces with words from the box.

play	can't	do	speak	live	can	love	I'm

Dear Marisol,

Thanks for your e-mail. _____ your new key-pal. My name is Cho Sun-Ah.

I _____ in Pusan, Korea. I'm a student at Pusan National University.

In my country, we _____ Korean. I study English at the university.

I _____ speak a little French, but I can't speak Spanish.

I _____ music too! I can't _____ any instruments,
but I can sing. I have lots of CDs. Who is your favorite singer?

I can ski a little, but I _____ play soccer or tennis. My favorite sport is
baseball. I always watch it on TV. _____ you like baseball?

Your friend,
Sun-Ah

D Write your answer to Marisol's e-mail. Answer Marisol's three questions.

Dear Marisol,

_____

_____

_____

_____

_____

_____

_____

_____

Your friend,

_____